CW01095362

A Career
in
Plumbing

A Career in Plumbing

by Carol Cannavan

First edition published 2016
Second edition published April 2018

This book's aim is to serve as a guide for someone interested in a career in the UK plumbing and heating industry. Although the advice and information in this book is believed to be accurate and true at the time of publication, the author cannot accept any legal responsibility or liability for any errors or omissions that may be made.

Follow Carol on Twitter
@PlumbCareer

ISBN-13: 978-1518688126
ISBN-10: 1518688128

CONTENTS

ABOUT THE AUTHOR

Carol Cannavan worked as a journalist and editor in the plumbing and heating industry for over 18 years. She was the communications manager for the Chartered Institute of Plumbing and Heating Engineering (CIPHE) and edited the Institute's journal, *P&HE Magazine*. She went on to be the editor of *HIP! Magazine*, which is distributed to plumbing students in colleges and training centres around the UK.

In her time spent working at the CIPHE, Carol was often interviewed on radio and appeared on *Richard and Judy* TV show to talk about diversity in the industry.

Currently, Carol edits and produces *The Woman Writer* on behalf of the Society of Women Writers & Journalists (SWWJ).

Carol is a Fellow of the SWWJ and is a Companion member of the CIPHE, the professional body for the plumbing and heating industry.

ACKNOWLEDGEMENTS

I would like to say a big 'thank you' to all the people who helped me with this book. Kevin Wellman and Danny Davis of the CIPHE were particularly helpful; Geoff Marsh MBE and Master Plumber Terry Fillary MBE have both been a great inspiration to me over the years. I'm grateful to Colin Topp for his constructive criticism and my final thanks go to my husband, Bill Cannavan, who qualified as a plumbing technician and became a senior consulting engineer – his advice has been invaluable!

FOREWORD

When considering a career in plumbing, remember that it is one of the oldest engineering services, serving people wherever they live, work, rest or play. That includes homes, hospitals, offices, factories, sports facilities, theatres, etc. In other words, wherever there are people, plumbing services will be on hand to support them.

Today, we have a rapidly increasing world population and a decreasing availability of drinking quality water; energy supplies need to be conserved and new products/technologies need to be developed. Plumbers and heating installers are going to play an important role in providing services that will help to overcome these issues.

In this authoritative book, plumbing and heating engineering career opportunities are described in detail and their scope should attract those with ambition to engage with a truly worthwhile and interesting occupation. Plumbing craftspeople, technicians and engineers are all equally satisfying vocations for those who wish to enter an area of challenging employment. We require men and women with a variety of educational backgrounds to safeguard the future of a key industry. This thoughtful collection of information is therefore a valuable work of reference.

Speaking from experience, I can say with conviction, that plumbing in its widest sense as a career is a great way of making a living.

Geoff Marsh MBE
Past Master of The Worshipful Company of Plumbers and Past President of the Chartered Institute of Plumbing and Heating Engineering

INTRODUCTION

I worked as a journalist and editor in the UK plumbing and heating industry for over 18 years. In that time I met people who were passionate about what they did... and I also met those who really shouldn't have been in the industry at all! That's what made me decide to write a book about a career in plumbing. I want the world to know about the fantastic opportunities there are in the industry (and the wonderful people you could meet!).

Just ask yourself one question – how would we thrive without plumbers looking after the health and safety of the nation? We depend on fresh drinking water for our survival and good sanitation to prevent the spread of disease. That's why it's so important that plumbers are fully qualified and have the right experience to deal with the problems that can arise in plumbing systems.

We only have to look back through history to see how improved sanitation over the centuries has prevented millions from dying, from either contaminated water or water borne diseases, such as cholera. Sadly, many countries in the third world still have to deal with these problems. According to the World Health Organisation, diarrhoeal diseases alone are responsible for the deaths of 2 million people every year and it's estimated that 88% of those deaths are attributable to unsafe water supply, sanitation and hygiene.

Over the years, the role of the plumber has changed considerably. 60 years ago a domestic plumber in the UK would mainly deal with the cold water supply, blocked drains, toilet repairs, replacing rainwater guttering and repairing leaky roofs; sometimes they replaced glass in leaded light windows. These days they tackle a huge range of jobs. Technologies have been developed that harness energy from the sun, sea, ground and air. A domestic plumber could be installing a solar thermal water heating system one day and repairing a boiler the next day. Of course, they still carry out the day-to-day work such as installing bathroom suites or repairing burst pipes, but the opportunities for diversifying have never been better. That's why a career in the plumbing and heating industry can be exciting and challenging.

You'll see as you progress through this book that the plumbing industry has a lot to offer in the way of careers and opportunities, but like all things it takes a lot of hard work to make it to the top. If you are determined you will find a way to overcome any barriers.

If you are still at school, I hope this book sparks your interest. If you are considering changing your career, I hope you find the answer to your questions.

There is a comprehensive list of organisations in chapter 14 that will not only help you to get a start in the industry, but will also assist you as your career progresses.

Good luck!

CHAPTER 1
ABOUT THE INDUSTRY

If you are looking for a job that will give you a living for life, then a career in the plumbing and heating industry could be the answer. Experienced and qualified plumbers will always be in demand because of the wide range of services they provide.

What does plumbing cover?

The word 'Plumbing' comes from the Latin word plumbum, which means lead. According to the Chartered Institute of Plumbing and Heating Engineering (CIPHE), the professional body for the industry, plumbing is defined as:

- The competent design, specification, installation and maintenance of all distribution and retrieval pipework systems for the transportation of fluids, both liquid and gaseous for domestic, non-domestic, industrial and medical facilities.

- The provision of relevant advice, selection and installation of all methods of energy generation and conservation.

- Ensuring that all terminal fittings, sanitary appliances, controls and equipment allow safe and efficient operation of systems, whilst protecting the environment and all individuals.

- The protection and preservation of buildings and structures against damage, due to ingress of rainwater by the application of suitable weathering materials.

It's a pretty comprehensive definition, but the first bullet point is the one to focus on. Most people are aware of the everyday jobs undertaken by a domestic plumber, such as installing bathroom suites, showers, toilets, washbasins, radiators and designing central heating systems. However, plumbers can also gain qualifications to install boilers and other heating appliances. Therefore, plumbers may be also known as plumbing engineers or plumbing and heating engineers/technicians, they are also known as plumbing and heating installers.

Plumbers cover work in the domestic, commercial and industrial sectors. There are a number of areas that plumbers can specialise in, such as teaching, renewable energy, plumbing design (public health) or conservational leadwork, but we will cover that later on in more detail.

How many plumbers are there?

It is difficult to give an accurate figure on this, estimates vary from different organisations from 85,000 to 95,000+ plumbers in the UK. A high proportion of domestic plumbers will be self-employed or running a small to medium sized enterprise (SME). Over the years, efforts have been made to encourage more women into the industry, but even so, less than 1% of plumbers are female. Many see it as a career that fits perfectly with family life, especially if they become self-employed. However, like any type of job that is normally male dominated, you need to be determined.

Nationally less than 3% of plumbers come from an ethnic minority background. However, it is anticipated that this figure will rise.

The construction industry

The construction industry is made up of many trades. Plumbers play an important part; their expertise ensures water supplies, heating and sanitation are brought into buildings and the waste is taken out. Besides the plumbers who 'work on the tools' (actually carrying out the plumbing work), there is a need for other plumbing professionals such as project engineers, designers, chargehands, consultants, specifiers and estimators.

So, once you have trained to be a plumber it could be just the beginning, as there are different roles that may interest you later on. Normally, you would need to have gained a certain amount of experience in the industry first and it may mean that you have to gain further qualifications, but you will find that hard work and dedication will be rewarded. (See chapter 9 for information on progressing in the industry.)

The environment

Energy efficiency and water conservation are two topics at the top of the agenda for the government. Fossil fuels (coal, oil and natural gas) could run out in less than fifty years time, so alternative energy options are needed. The same goes for creating products that help to conserve water. It's hard to believe, but the UK has less available water per person than many other European countries, including France, Italy and Greece.

Water shortages in the past have prompted new measures to combat the problem. The government is trying to encourage rainwater harvesting and grey water recycling (wastewater generated from domestic processes such as dish washing, laundry and bathing). Manufacturers are doing their bit by producing products that help to conserve water, such as showers that restrict water flow, without effecting showering performance.

The need to protect our environment has driven many changes in legislation and regulations that affect the plumbing and heating industry in the UK.

The government has been concerned by climate change for some time, particularly the effects caused by the huge amount of carbon dioxide that is being released into the atmosphere. Households produce a substantial amount of CO_2 through heating and producing hot water, so this has brought in regulations that concentrate on energy efficiency.

These regulations have helped to cut carbon emissions substantially, but there is still some way to go. Europe's climate targets of cutting carbon emissions by 40 per cent by 2030 and 60 per cent by 2050, means that more 'green' technologies will have to be installed in the future to cut emissions further.

In the mean time, heating manufacturers have developed boilers that run very efficiently and produce less CO_2. There are also heat recovery systems that can save up to 17% of the energy used in heating water.

The industry is continually researching and developing new products and technologies. This means that a skilled work-force is needed to advise consumers on the best options for them.

Following Regulations

All plumbers have to abide by Water and Building Regulations. They are in place to ensure that standards are met and to protect the health and safety of the public. Contravention can lead to prosecution and the possible imposition of substantial fines.

Regulations are reviewed and updated to take into account new legislation, which might affect the construction industry. Water Regulations are enforced by the Water Authorities and Building Regulations by Building Control officers.

The demand for plumbers

As mentioned earlier, there will always be a de
professional plumbers – especially when the econom, _
growing. New housing developments and interest from
commercial enterprises to build new businesses in the UK
will fuel the demand. There is a huge housing shortage and
the government is doing all it can to encourage growth in
the construction industry.

The recession had a huge impact on new housing
developments over the last few years. In 2013, the
construction of 109,370 new homes was completed in
England – the lowest figure for four years. To put that into
perspective, the number of households is expected to grow
by 221,000 every year this decade.

On the domestic side, there is always a steady stream
of work such as: installing or maintaining heating systems,
repairing or installing sanitation systems, fitting domestic
appliances (such as dishwashers), etc. On top of that, if the
economy is thriving homeowners will be more likely to
extend their property and will be looking to either add
bathrooms, shower rooms, extend kitchens, or revamp the
existing sanitaryware.

Skills shortages

There has been talk of a skills shortage in the plumbing
industry for many years. However, it's not the fact that
there aren't enough plumbers, it's more to do with the skill
level of the plumbers.

Unfortunately, the name 'plumber' isn't protected like it is
in some professions, such as solicitors. This means anyone
can advertise their services as a plumber and start up in
business, even if they do not have any qualifications. This
has caused lots of problems, as these individuals do not
have the knowledge or experience needed to carry out
a wide range of plumbing work. In countries such as

Germany, America and Australia, plumbers have to be licenced by law.

Beware of rogue ('fast-track') training courses, they are usually unsuitable for someone wanting a career in the industry. Some of these courses last just a few weeks and can cost thousands of pounds. The trouble is employers are not interested in the qualifications gained from these courses. You'll find this message repeated throughout this book because it is so important.

There are no shortcuts to becoming a professional plumber. We will be looking at the qualifications recognised by the industry in chapter 8.

CHAPTER 2
WHAT MAKES A GOOD PLUMBER?

There are a number of key skills needed to become a plumber. Maths and science play their part, but your personality and the way you interact with people are also important.

In this chapter we are going to look at the skills and qualities that will help you to be a good plumber. You might think that most of them are obvious, but some may surprise you. Don't be put off by the length of the list – it's just meant as a guide. If you are still at school or college you might not yet have developed many of the qualities or skills mentioned, but no doubt in time you will.

An employer will be looking for many of the following attributes – how do you think you will fare?

APPROACHABILITY: Do you have a friendly, outgoing personality? This is very important when it comes to dealing with customers and the people you work with. Being polite, friendly and understanding will help you build a good reputation.

COMMUNICATION SKILLS: It's extremely important to be able to express yourself and get your point across, either verbally or in written form. This applies to any job you do. Equally, you need to be able to listen and act upon instructions that might be quite complicated.

Don't be despondent if you feel you have a weakness in this area. Literacy is a core skill and colleges will have courses that will help you to improve your standard of English.

CONCENTRATION: Are you easily distracted? Lack of concentration can cause accidents, as well as make it difficult to successfully complete whatever you are working on. When studying you will need to totally focus on the coursework and put aside any distractions. When working on a job, always give it your full attention.

CURIOSITY: Are you curious about how things work, or how they are put together? If you are, it will definitely be an advantage in training to become a plumber.

DEPENDABILITY: Are you reliable? Your employer will not be happy if he/she cannot depend on you to be at work on time. When it comes to domestic plumbers, one of the top complaints from consumers is that the plumber does not arrive on time, or in some cases not at all. You must be responsible for your actions; if you know you are going to be late for an appointment make sure you notify the customer and be realistic with the estimate of the time it will take you to arrive.

ENTHUSIASM: Employers are looking for motivated staff who are enthusiastic about the work they do. If you show drive and energy, it won't go unnoticed! However, if you don't turn up for work on time, or fail to turn up at all... you will soon be looking for a new job.

HONESTY AND INTEGRITY: These are very important attributes. Always be 'up front' with what work you will carry out and how much it will cost. If anything unforeseen crops up let the customer know straight away. To do well in business you need to build a good reputation – this should be based on honesty and integrity, as well as your level of skill. If customers think you did a good job and were honest with them, it's likely that they will recommend you (or the company you are working for) to their friends and family. This type of publicity is priceless.

PHYSICAL FITNESS: You need to be quite fit to be a plumber. The work can be strenuous and the working day can often be long. Besides strength you'll need to be agile, as you often have to get into tight spaces. Always follow health and safety regulations when it comes to lifting heavy objects, such as boilers. Otherwise you could end up injuring yourself. On the plus side, plumbing materials these days are a lot lighter than they were years ago, so if you are generally fit and in good health, dealing with day-to-day work shouldn't be a problem. It may be a good idea to join a gym if you feel you need to work on your stamina.

PROBLEM SOLVING: Are you the type of person who likes solving puzzles? If you are, this will be a big help. Plumbers often have to find solutions for difficult installations or work out why an appliance or piece of equipment isn't working properly. It will also be very helpful if you have visualisation skills, where you can picture in your mind layouts and plans and how everything fits together. Being good at maths is a bonus as a lot of the work centres around measurements and calculations.

TEAM PLAYER: It's important to be able to work well with others and follow orders. This is essential on construction sites where there is a need for people with different skills to work together. Bricklayers, ground workers, plasterers, electricians, plumbers, glaziers, carpenters, painters and decorators, would all be involved in a new build, although not all at the same time.

Feeling confident?

Hopefully, you have mentally ticked off all those qualities and feel you have what it takes to become a good plumber.

Now read through the list of additional qualities that will help you to become a great plumber!

APPEARANCE: Just a little bit of thought about how others might see you, will help you to give the right impression (especially important when being interviewed!). It's human nature to judge people by their appearance, so clean overalls, boots and a tidy hairstyle will go a long way to make you look business-like. It might be unfair, but if you turn up for work looking scruffy you will give the impression that you don't care much about what you do. If you use a van, that should also be kept clean. Of course, if you work on a building site, then it is expected that you will get dirty and your appearance doesn't matter so much. However, you will be required to wear Personal Protective Equipment (PPE).

ADAPTABILITY: Are you flexible in the way you work? Sometimes you may be pulled from one job and expected to take over unfinished work elsewhere. Could you adapt easily in this type of situation? Also, you may have to be flexible in the hours you work, as you may be required to do shift work.

COMMON SENSE: Are you good at understanding and judging situations? Most people have a natural ability to do this, but some lack common sense. However, if you have a logical mind you will find that this will help you to see problems that might arise.

CONFIDENCE: A confident person gains everyone's trust, whether it's to do with quoting for work or dealing with an emergency. However, confidence is not something that can be learned like a set of rules; confidence is a state of mind. If you feel that you are lacking in confidence don't worry too much, because positive thinking, knowledge and experience should help to improve or boost your confidence levels.

DEXTERITY: Plumbing is a craft and the more practice you get at carrying out the different elements of plumbing jobs, the quicker and more skilled you will become. Being 'good with your hands' will help you to master the skill sets needed to become a good plumber. As the old saying goes, 'practice makes perfect!'

METHODICAL ATTITUDE: By tackling your work step by step you should reduce the likelihood of mistakes. This will definitely benefit you whilst you are training. In time you will learn to prioritise tasks, this will enable you to deal with the most important elements first. Being methodical will ensure jobs are carried out carefully and thoroughly.

PERSEVERANCE: Although you will be working with similar materials each day, you'll find that most plumbing and heating jobs differ, because systems are rarely the same in buildings. This will inevitably bring up problems that can be very frustrating to deal with, but perseverance will help you to overcome the obstacles. The main thing is not to be put off by unpredictable situations – keep calm and think it through logically.

PROFESSIONALISM: Being professional is essential if you want to build a good reputation for yourself, whatever sector you work in. A professional attitude in your work will create a good impression; this will help you to gain respect from others.

You will also need to invest time in keeping your skills up to date by attending training courses, seminars, talks, etc. This is known as Continuing Professional Development (CPD).

SAFETY MINDSET: It's important to know how to use equipment correctly and to give your full attention to the job you are carrying out. Carelessness can result in fires, flooding or explosions! You also need to be careful when it comes to lifting heavy objects, so you don't damage your spine or joints.

TIME MANAGEMENT: It's very important to be able to work out how much time it will take to complete tasks. Domestic plumbers have to give estimates to customers that give an accurate costing of the job. You could find that you are working for less if you do not get this right. If someone else employs you, they will not be happy that you are losing them money!

WILLINGNESS TO LEARN: Besides gaining qualifications, you will be expected to carry out CPD throughout your career. It is important to keep up to date with new technologies, products and regulations affecting the industry.

Still interested?

Remember, it can take years to qualify, so you will have lots of time to develop your skills and improve yourself. In that time your confidence will grow and you'll have the experience needed to become a good plumber.

In the next chapter we will be looking at the apprenticeship route into the industry.

CHAPTER 3
APPRENTICESHIPS

Introduction

An apprenticeship is a work-based training programme that offers paid employment while you learn. The main benefit is being able to gain valuable work experience, while you are developing all the practical and technical skills needed to become a competent plumber. An apprenticeship in the plumbing and heating industry is a great way to start your career.

Who can apply for an apprenticeship?

If you are still at senior school, it is an ideal time to consider applying for an apprenticeship in the plumbing and heating industry. You have to be at least 16 to apply. At present, the government covers the full cost of your course until you are 19, after that, your employer covers the cost for those who are 19 or older.

If you have already attended college and gained A-Level qualifications, a career in plumbing is still a good choice. After successfully completing your plumbing courses, it would be easier for you to take the next step on to an appropriate degree course. This would enable you to gain professional recognition with the Engineering Council as a Chartered Engineer. Apprenticeships in the plumbing and heating industry are open to all genders.

How long does an apprenticeship take?

To become fully qualified can take up to four years. The first part of the apprenticeship will cover NVQ Level 2 Diploma (Modern Apprenticeships in Scotland), and then you will progress on to the Advanced Apprenticeship in order to gain the NVQ Level 3 Diploma. In 2018 it might then be a qualification relating to the Trailblazer Plumbing and Domestic Heating Technician Apprenticeship (see page 19).

Entry qualifications?

You will usually need four GCSEs at C grade or above, but it's best to check this out with the college that you want to attend as requirements do vary. Most colleges will ask you to take an assessment test before you are enrolled (see chapter 7 for sample questions). Sometimes an interview is also required.

How much does an apprentice earn?

All apprentices must receive the appropriate national minimum wage. The hourly rate increased to £3.70 per hour for apprentices in April 2018. This may not sound a lot, but when you consider that your course has been paid for and you are gaining valuable skills and experience, it's not a bad deal, especially when a university course could cost around £9,000 per year! As a minimum, you can expect to earn around £100 per week, but some companies may be more generous.

What can I earn when I qualify?

This is a tricky question to answer because it depends on a lot of things. The first is location. Obviously, someone working in a city or busy town will expect to earn more than someone working in a more rural environment. Likewise, someone working for a big company will expect to earn more than someone working for a small business, where you are perhaps the only employee.

When you first qualify, you can expect to earn between £15k-£20k. As you gain more experience in the industry this will obviously rise, so you can expect to earn between £25k-£35k. Of course, there are always exceptions and bonuses may be involved.

How many hours will I work?

You will work approximately 30 hours per week and spend a day (possibly two) at college. The working day may start at 8am.

Holidays?

Apprentices are entitled to 20 days of paid holiday per year, plus bank holidays.

How do I apply?

To get an apprenticeship, you need an employer. This can be done through a training provider, such as JTL Training. They will liaise with you, the college and your employer to make sure you are on track with your studies.

Here are some of the ways you can help yourself to contact companies that are involved in apprenticeship schemes.

- Call the National Careers Service on 0800 100 900. They will advise you on your options and will give you information about finding a job. It's also worth visiting their website as they have a list of vacancies.

- Get in touch with organisations such as CITB (Construction Industry Training Board) and BESA (Building Engineering Services Association).

- The NotGoingToUni website has a substantial list of apprenticeship vacancies, but it does cover all industries so it may take a while to find just what you are looking for. Visit: **www.notgoingtouni.co.uk**

- Check out the recruitment section of local newspapers to see if any companies are advertising apprenticeship vacancies.

- Search the internet for companies that you would like to work for, to see if they are advertising apprenticeship opportunities.

- Get in touch directly with a company you would like to work for. Take a copy of your CV with you and ask them to keep it on file in case a vacancy arises.

- Ask family and friends if they know of anyone who is looking for an apprentice.

In chapter 14 there are lists of useful websites and contact details that will lead to more information on apprenticeships and training.

What will I learn?

As a plumbing apprentice, you'll learn about the installation and maintenance of plumbing systems and components, along with health and safety. As you progress, you will be working under minimal supervision to complete the installation and maintenance of domestic hot water, cold water, sanitation, drainage, rainwater systems, central heating systems and components.

As a first year plumbing apprentice you can expect to spend at least one day a week at college and the rest of the time you will be working for your employer. A good deal of time will be spent watching how jobs are carried out and carrying materials and tools for the plumber. You will be involved in cutting pipes and soldering.

However, as you get more knowledgeable you will be given more tasks to do. This could include first fixings – fitting all of the main pipes, and second fixings – fitting radiators and bathroom suites. Hours will vary, but you can expect to work from around 8am to 4pm.

On the Advanced Level Apprenticeship, your skill base will broaden and you will able to plan and carry out a variety of installations including:

- Complex cold water systems
- Domestic hot water
- Sanitation and drainage systems
- Gas central heating systems

You will also be able to commission, service and maintain those systems.

Apprenticeships in the Armed Forces

You may want to consider applying for an Engineering Apprenticeship in the British Army or Royal Navy. This may appeal if you are looking for a career that also brings the chance to travel and to experience a completely different way of life. In these organisations plumbers/engineers are trained to set up equipment to supply fresh water and provide sanitation in a variety of situations and places. However, a word of caution here, this could well include disaster areas and war zones!

The British Army is probably the best option if you want to train specifically as a plumber, with skills that would transfer more easily into civilian life.

Army apprenticeships are part of a nationally recognised scheme, giving soldiers the chance to work for an employer at the same time as studying for a relevant, work-based qualification.

Each apprenticeship fits in with military training and is closely related to a soldier's Army role, so as well as becoming a better soldier, they are working towards a qualification that will be valued by civilian employers. Apprenticeships in the Army are delivered on full pay.

There are two apprenticeship levels:

• **Apprenticeship Level 2**

Level 2 apprenticeships are equivalent to five good GCSE passes. Military trade training forms the core of this level. A range of key-skills qualifications (including literacy and numeracy) are completed and a technical certificate is gained. By the end of the apprenticeship, soldiers are skilled Army tradesman and are rewarded with an NVQ Level 2 Diploma.

• **Advanced Apprenticeship Level 3**

Level 3 apprenticeships are equivalent to two A-level passes. These apprenticeships apply to the Army's technical trades. Advanced apprentices gain the relevant technical certificates through their trade training, as well as an NVQ Level 3 Diploma and key skills. To qualify for an advanced apprenticeship, five GCSEs at grade C or above are required. Alternatively, a Level 2 Army apprenticeship is acceptable.

Traineeships

In August 2013, the government brought in training programmes for young people that would support them in developing skills, that would help them to gain an apprenticeship. These programmes are called Traineeships.

What is a traineeship?

A traineeship is an education and training programme with work experience, that is focused on giving young people the skills and experience that employers are looking for. Basically, they help young people to become 'work ready' before they go on to do an apprenticeship. An important part of this is to develop maths and English skills.

Traineeships are delivered by training providers and funded by the government, with employers providing the valuable work experience placement as part of the programme. Unlike apprenticeships, the trainee will not be paid a wage. The training programme can last up to six months and gives the trainee the opportunity to see if they are suited to the job.

All young people undertaking a traineeship will be required to study English and maths, unless they have achieved:

- GCSE A* - C in those subjects or, for those aged 19-23,
- GCSE A* - C in those subjects or a functional skills qualification at Level 2.

A full Level 2 qualification is equivalent to 5 GCSEs at Grades A* - C and a full Level 3 qualification is equivalent to 2 or more A-level passes.

Trailblazer Apprenticeships

In October 2013, the government announced that it wanted to reform apprenticeships, so that they are more rigorous and responsive to the needs of employers. These new schemes are called 'Trailblazer' Apprenticeships and are being developed for a number of industries.

In October 2014, the Department for Business, Innovation & Skills (BIS), announced the development of a Plumbing and Domestic Heating Technician Trailblazer Apprenticeship in England.

There are a number of changes that will be made to the present system. For instance, students will be assessed in a different way and they will be graded at the end of training. They must also be able to meet professional registration requirements for Engineering Technician (EngTech) status with the Engineering Council.

Employers, professional bodies and trade associations are developing the new standard for the plumbing and heating industry. It is anticipated that the course for the Trailblazer Apprenticeship will be in place by September 2018.

It's not just the structure of apprenticeships that is changing. There will also be a change in the way apprenticeship schemes are funded. Although at the time of writing this book the government was reviewing feedback from schemes already in place in different industries. The government wants Trailblazer-developed standards to be in place for all occupations as soon as possible.

Putting together a CV

If you have never had a job, you are probably wondering what to include in your CV. Honesty is definitely the best policy. There is no point in lying about your skills or qualifications, because at some point it's very likely that you will be found out!

You'll need to put your name, address and contact details at the top of the CV. Then, break it up into headings, like Personal Statement, Key Skills, Education, Work Experience (that's if you have had a part-time or Saturday job), Hobbies or Interests.

In the Personal Statement section you need to sell yourself, so include positive things like: hard working, motivated, willing to learn, etc. Don't be frightened to mention things that show you know you have areas to work on such as: 'I was disappointed in the grade I got in maths, but I am determined to work hard in this area'.

When it comes to listing your skills, don't forget to include things like IT. An employer may be very interested in your ability to use Microsoft Office programmes, as well as your knowledge of social media/building websites, as that could be used to promote business.

When it comes to hobbies or interests, if you play football/netball or any sports, do include them. This will show you are a team player and are relatively fit. Also, if you are involved with hobbies like building models, gardening or anything where you are using your hands/tools, it will go in your favour.

If you have finished your apprenticeship and are looking for a job that will help with your career progression, don't forget to mention if you have entered any skills competitions, won any awards, or are a member of a professional body (see page 54).

If you do a search on the internet, you'll find sites like www.reed.co.uk that help you to build a CV for free (check out their school leaver template).

CHAPTER 4
CASE STUDIES

Case Study One:

Ryan Hill (19) has completed just over two years as an apprentice plumber and works for a small company near to where he lives in Surrey.

It took a while for Ryan to find an employer to take him on as an apprentice. He started out by looking on the internet for local plumbing and heating companies. He sent them a letter explaining that he was looking for an apprenticeship and enclosed his CV and a stamped addressed envelope for a reply. Even though he approached around 30 companies, he didn't receive a single response.

"I was very disappointed," said Ryan, "but I knew I wanted to be a plumber and wasn't going to give up."

His next step was to select a number of companies that he would like to work for and went to see them, personally handing over a copy of his CV. This did the trick – he was invited to spend a trial week with a small plumbing company to see how he would fit in.

Ryan enjoyed the time he spent with the company. He got on well with the staff and was keen to help as much as he could. At the end of the week he was called in to see the boss.

"Apparently I made a good impression, because I was offered a job. I remember feeling elated – so pleased with myself."

Since joining the company as an apprentice, Ryan has attended college one day a week and shadows plumbers, developing his skills as he goes along. He has one more year before he completes his apprenticeship and becomes fully qualified.

"I really enjoy the variety of the work. One day I can be helping to fit a bathroom suite, the next I'm involved with renewables. Some of the coursework has been tough, but I have overcome it. I have no regrets – this is the job for me."

Case Study Two:

Josh Roberts (18) wasn't sure what he wanted to do for a living. He knew he liked working with his hands, but it wasn't until a plumber came to his parent's house in Derby to fit a new central heating system, that he became interested in plumbing.

"Looking back, I must have been a bit of a pain as I kept asking the plumber (Phil) what he was doing and why he was doing it. He was very patient and explained everything as he went along."

After the installation was completed, Phil asked Josh if he would like to help him out on a few jobs. Josh didn't hesitate and arranged to meet up with Phil the following week. He enjoyed every minute of the time spent helping out, so when he was offered an apprenticeship he accepted straight away.

"Phil had been mainly working on his own for a number of years, he was thinking of taking on someone to train and I happened to be in the right place at the right time."

Josh attends college for one day a week and spends the rest of the time out with Phil. He has completed the first year of his NVQ Level 2 Diploma course and is looking forward to going back to his second year.

"I've made some good mates at college. A couple of the lads I started with have dropped out, which is a big shame. I could tell one of them wasn't really committed and the other was struggling with the theory. I've always been fascinated by how things work and I hate to be beaten by anything – I'm sure this has helped me.

"Phil is a great bloke to work for. He's been a plumber for 20 years and I've learnt so much from him. I'd like to think I've also contributed to the business, as I've helped him to set up a website and we now use social media to promote the business."

CHAPTER 5
CHANGING CAREERS

Often it's the case that someone who starts out on one career path ends up on another. It's not unusual to find people enrolling on plumbing courses in their 20s, 30s or 40s, but it can present problems for them. For a start, mature students will usually have to pay their own course fees.

Work Experience

Another hurdle is getting work experience, without this you cannot complete the NVQ Level 2/3 Diplomas – and without these qualifications it will be hard to gain employment in the plumbing and heating industry.

Helping yourself

If the college/training centre can't help with work experience, you could try contacting local plumbing companies to see if they are looking to train someone. It has to be said that the majority will be SMEs (small or medium enterprises), often just sole traders. Some may welcome a more mature employee who shows dedication, commitment and can be relied upon. However, others may view you as a future competitor, especially if your goal is to set up in business for yourself.

Ask around your family and friends to see if they know anyone in the trade who might give you a chance. If you have transferable skills, such as plastering or tiling, it will put you in a favourable light.

It might be worth visiting local plumbing merchants to see if they have a notice board. Ask if you can have a space to put up some details about yourself.

Social media can sometimes be a good tool to use. If you have a Facebook account, why not promote yourself on there? Put together a short snappy profile about yourself, giving information such as the skills you can offer and if you have a clean driving licence. Ask your Facebook friends to share, it's amazing how many people could end up seeing your request for work experience/job. You could also use Twitter, but make sure you state the area that you live in.

Some sole traders or small plumbing businesses may be inclined to offer work experience, providing they don't have to pay you. Whether you take up such an offer will be down to your financial situation.

Earnings

Another drawback to entering training as a mature student is the money you are likely to earn. It's unlikely that your employer will want to pay you very much to start with. If you have a mortgage or a family, would you be able to survive on a minimum wage?

CSCS cards

It's important to note that most principal contractors and major house builders, require construction workers (even labourers) on their sites to hold a valid Construction Skills Certification Scheme (CSCS) card. Trainees and apprentices can apply for a card, but they have to prove their knowledge of health and safety. Full details can be found on the CSCS website.

Choosing your course

Do as much research as possible. Contact your local FE college, technical college, or training centre to find out if they have a plumbing department. If they do, try to find out if they can help with work experience – some colleges have contacts with local employers.

Private training companies

Google or other search engines will bring up lists of private training providers offering plumbing and heating qualifications. Going down this route may suit some people as there isn't the 'tie-in' of academic start dates, term times, etc., although it would normally cost more than enrolling on a college course. Also, adult learners often prefer a little more of a 'mature' learning environment, compared to that provided by some colleges.

A word of warning here though – like most things there are good and bad training providers. Even though some will have excellent facilities, they may not offer industry-recognised qualifications. You could end up very disappointed, with a chunk of money missing from your savings. Do as much research as possible before committing to any courses, including finding out if the tutors/assessors have themselves achieved NVQ Level 3 qualifications and have industry experience.

Fast-track courses

Some training centres offer fast-track courses to become a qualified plumber, which will only take weeks/months to achieve. These should be avoided – be especially wary if they suggest you will earn £50-75k as soon as you qualify! On the whole, the fast-track courses that are offered are extremely expensive and do not result in an industry-recognised NVQ Level 2/3 Diploma, which can take a couple of years to gain. These qualifications are work-based, which can only be assessed once someone has undertaken work experience.

Make sure you read the small print – some training providers say they will help to get you work experience… but they don't guarantee it. Some will only give 'work placements', which can lead to the student being ill prepared for assessment, as they can be put in with a company at short notice to do their 'observed tasks'. Unscrupulous training centres have been known to sign off inexperienced and potentially incompetent plumbers.

Also, they might advertise the fact that their training centre is City & Guilds approved (or any other awarding organisation), but this does not necessarily mean that the course on offer is the industry-recognised plumbing course that will lead to a worthwhile qualification (see chapter 8).

Fast-track courses are usually very big on theory and offer some practical work (normally in the training centre), but to be proficient it literally takes years to develop these skills – a couple of months are practically useless. Imagine going to a dentist who had read up on dental work, but only spent a few weeks practising. Would you let him drill your teeth? Manual skills are learned through repetition. You need a thorough grounding in theory and practical work; that along with work experience will provide you with the skills you need to become a professional plumber. There are no shortcuts!

That said, if you are looking for 'add on' qualifications, such as Water Regulations or Hot Water Systems and Safety courses, etc., a private training centre could be ideal. Likewise, if you have experience in the industry but lack qualifications, this could also be the route for you.

CHAPTER 6
CASE STUDIES

Case Study Three:

Sarah Cordell (32) had worked in retail for ten years and was managing an Off Licence, when she decided to change careers.

She lived in a rented property, which had various plumbing problems from the drainage constantly blocking to the boiler needing replacing. Sarah always thought of herself as a practical type of person – this made her think about training to become a plumber/heating engineer.

"I wasn't happy in my job and was looking for a career that would be a challenge. Plumbing certainly filled that gap!"

It wasn't easy going back to college, but Sarah said she was very fortunate in the support she was given by her friends and family. Luckily, the flexible hours she worked at the Off Licence allowed her to attend the course, so she was still earning money.

"Everyone seemed to think it was a really good career choice for me, which helped me take the first step and apply for a place on the ASET Level 1 Plumbing course."

Sarah was the only girl on the course, but she got on well with the other students and the lecturers. It was around this time that a heating engineer arrived at her rented property to install a new boiler. She took the opportunity to ask for career advice and Ray offered her the chance to work for him one day a week, unpaid, for some experience. This helped her to progress on to the Level 2 course. Then, when Sarah was made redundant from her retail job, Ray offered to take her on full-time, with a day off for college. She went on to gain a Level 3 City & Guilds qualification.

Sarah has been working with Ray for over six years. She successfully completed a course to get her ACS gas qualification and is now Gas Safe registered. She loves the job and the variety of work it brings. Sarah also gained a City & Guilds Level 3 Award in the Requirements for Electrical Installations, which covers the 17th Edition.

"No job is the same and with the industry constantly evolving, I'll always have something new to learn. The physical side of the job has been a bit of a challenge, as I'm only small and quite slight with it. I've had to bulk up with weights in order to ensure that nuts are tight enough on rad valves and tap connectors. On the plus side, I find it easier to get under the floor to find leaks on pipework and I fit easily into tight spaces under sinks."

Case Study Four:

Tracey Richardson was a weapons technician in the Royal Air Force for 22 years. After her service, she did a two-day 'taster' plumbing course, as one of the short courses taken during her resettlement training. Initially she was going to become a tutor for adults with learning difficulties, as she gained a Postgraduate Certificate in Education (PGCE) for Specialists in Learning Difficulties whilst in the RAF, but when the resettlement clerk piped up, 'You'll never be short of work as a female plumber', the seed was sown!

It took Tracey five years from starting her NVQ Level 2, to completing Level 3. In that time she endeavoured to get as much experience as possible via contacts she had made from her RAF days. After qualifying, Tracey worked on the tools for three years before teaching part-time at South Staffordshire College. In 2011 she joined a private training company as a full-time lecturer and assessor.

"I really enjoy teaching – especially those who want to be taught! It is nice when students thank you for the time and effort you put in to helping them. On the other hand, there are some individuals who initially appear too casual about their training and then realise they are starting to struggle. Once they acknowledge that you are there to help and what you are saying does make sense, they start to respond and interact more. It's great to watch them flourish through their journey."

Tracey would like to see more females coming into the industry. She has been involved with 'women only' courses, which have been a big success. She has some advice for girls considering a career in plumbing and heating.

"What is stopping you? Having been out there on the tools myself and having trained and mentored many other women now actively earning a living as plumbers, there is always plenty of room for others."

One thing that annoys Tracey is the fast-track courses that some training centres offer. She believes it has done the industry no end of damage, as well as given false hope (and empty bank accounts!) to those who have enrolled.

"We do not offer fast-track courses as they serve no purpose. Yes, people want to get qualified and earning as soon as possible, that is understandable. However, if they have no real experience and limited knowledge of why they are doing certain tasks, it can potentially prove costly for them as well as their customers when things go wrong."

Note:

At present, Tracey is Vice President of the Chartered Institute of Plumbing and Heating Engineering (CIPHE). She takes on her role as President in June 2018. She will be the first woman to achieve this honour.

CHAPTER 7
ASSESSMENT TEST

It's quite likely that you will have to sit an assessment test before you gain a place on a plumbing course. There is a very good reason for this. The results of the test show whether you have the aptitude to become a qualified plumber.

The assessment paper will normally cover literacy skills, numerical skills and applied science and mathematical aptitude. It will usually take around an hour and a half to complete. Additionally, you may also be given a colour blindness test. It is possible that you may not be allowed to join the course if you are colour blind. The reason for this is because pipes are often colour coded. Also, many plumbers gain extra qualifications to tackle the electrical side of the job – this would involve colour coded wiring.

The following questions will give you some idea of what to expect for the literacy and numerical element, although the multi-choice answers may not always apply. There will also be questions relating to graphs, measurements and images. The staff at your local library should be able to help you choose some books that will help you brush up on your English and maths.

LITERACY

Write the correct spelling for the words that have been underlined in the following sentences.

1) The <u>pain</u> of glass was too big for the window.
2) <u>Their</u> are five books missing from the shelf.
3) I'm looking forward to the tea <u>brake</u>.
4) She snipped the thread holding the <u>seem</u> together.
5) Where have you <u>bin</u> today?

One word in each of the following sentences has been written incorrectly. Write the correct word.

6) The girl had been very pourly since her operation.
7) Call an ambulance, this is an emergincy!
8) The house was spotles before the children came home.
9) How much mony have you got left in the bank account?
10) After running frew the field he sat on a bench feeling exhausted.

Choose one of the four words shown in brackets to correctly finish the sentence.

11) My (fiend – phrend – friend – freind) gave me a great present.
12) I can't believe that you are (forty – fourty – forti – foorty) years old.
13) The job came with a great (celery – calary – salery – salary).
14) He is a man of great (currage – courage – curidge – currige).
15) This is a bit (worring – wurrying – worrying – whorrying).

Read the text below and then answer questions 16 – 20, choosing the word which describes the situation best.

<u>Report on Boiler</u>

Four days before Christmas, Mrs Preston's boiler broke down. It was covered by breakdown protection insurance and the insurer sent an engineer out the following day to repair it. All appeared to be well until the evening of Christmas day, when the boiler stopped working again.

The engineer sent out by the insurer two days later, told Mrs Preston that a new pump was needed. Unfortunately, the exact model required was not in stock and would have to be specially ordered. He did not know how long this would take and he said that some delay was inevitable because of office and warehouse closures over the holiday period.

Mrs Preston was distraught to learn this. She said she could not manage without hot water and central heating. Several members of her family were staying with her over the Christmas and New Year break, including her elderly mother.

16) What did the insurance protect against? (disasters – leaking – breakdown – snow).

17) The boiler broke down on Christmas day in the (morning – afternoon – evening – early hours).

18) The problem with the central heating system had left Mrs Preston feeling (sad – unwell – distressed – unhappy).

19) How many days before Christmas did the engineer visit Mrs Preston? (one – two – three – four).

20) The engineer had no (patience – control – say – hope) over the delay in ordering the pump.

NUMERACY

1) Which of these numbers shows fifty four thousand five hundred and twenty six? (545,026 – 54,526 – 5,450,026 – 54,500,26).

2) Round this number to the nearest hundred – 459.

3) Daniel managed to get a 15% discount on a £2,000 second-hand van. How much did he pay? (£1,555 – £1,600 – £1,700 – £1,755).

4) 15 x 3 + 19 – 31 = (which answer is correct: 44 – 38 – 33 – 31).

5) 105 – 37 x 4 + 28 = (which answer is correct: 300 – 305 – 307 – 308).

6) 20, 22, 26, 32 ___ 50 (what is the missing number in the sequence? 38 – 40 – 44 – 48).

7) 7, 14, 28, 56, 112 ___ (what is the next number in the sequence? 196 – 204 – 224 – 240).

8) Dave earns £200 per week and gives one fifth to his mum. How much does he give her? (£25 – £30 – £35 – £40).

9) John bought a tool set for £75 and sold it after adding 20% to the price. How much did he sell it for? (£85 – £90 – £95 – £100).

10) Which is the smallest number? (0.05 – 0.055 – 0.5 – 0.50).

11) What is the perimeter of a floor, 6 metres long and 3 metres wide? (14m – 16m – 18m – 20m).

12) What is the area of a floor, 8 metres long and 4 metres wide? (30^2 – 32^2 – 34^2 – 36^2).

13) Multiply 11.007 by 108.2 (1170.96 – 1180.86 – 1190.96 – 1196.09).

14) Divide 1064 by 8 (128 – 131 – 133 – 138).

15) Subtract 56.078 from 87.64 (30.65 – 31.56 – 32.65 – 33.56).

16) Subtract 1026 from 2003 (873 – 933 – 973 – 977).

17) Add the following numbers: 14, 108, 1027, 6, 339 (1409 – 1494 – 1499 – 1501).

18) Add the following numbers, 1.06, 113.94, 0.642, 2.009 (111.561 – 111.651 – 117.561 – 117.651).

19) What is one tenth of forty per cent? (4.0% – 4.4% – 4.5% – 4.7%).

20) What is half of fifty per cent? (15% – 20% – 25% – 30%).

1) Spacial awareness: Which image can be made from the three shapes below?

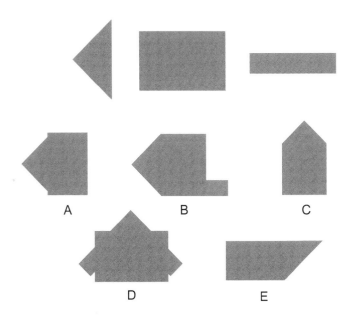

2) Mirror images: Which answer shows a reflection of the image below?

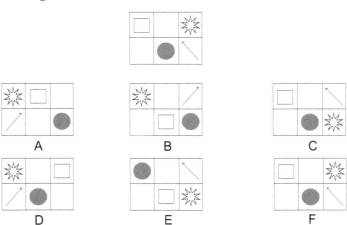

These questions are just to give you an idea of what might be included in an assessment test and are not intended as anything other than an exercise.

As mentioned before, it's a good idea to visit your library and ask the staff to recommend some suitable books. Alternatively, try searching the internet for samples of assessment papers for plumbing courses.

Here are the answers to the questions.

ANSWERS (Literacy)

1) pane 2) There 3) break 4) seam 5) been 6) poorly
7) emergency 8) spotless 9) money 10) through
11) friend 12) forty 13) salary 14) courage 15) worrying
16) breakdown 17) evening 18) distressed 19) three 20) control

ANSWERS (Numeracy)

1) 54,526 2) 500 3) £1,700 4) 33 5) 300 6) 40 7) 224
8) £40 9) £90 10) 0.05 11) 18m 12) 32^2 13) 1190.96 14)
133 15) 31.56 16) 977 17) 1494 18) 117.651 19) 4.0% 20)
25%

ANSWERS (Visuals)

1) C

2) D

Note: If you are dyslexic do let the college know, as they will allow you extra time to take the assessment.

CHAPTER 8
TRAINING AND QUALIFICATIONS

Is the idea of training to become a plumber beginning to appeal to you? If you are entering the trade via an apprenticeship or traineeship, your employer or training provider will advise you about the qualifications and courses you need to take. For those who are considering changing their careers, you'll find information on lots of options available to you in this chapter. There will also be information on professional qualifications.

Contact details of all the organisations mentioned in this section can be found in chapter 14.

Training over the years

Training for plumbers over the years has changed considerably, but you may be surprised how far back apprenticeships go. It's documented that plumbers served a seven-year apprenticeship back in 1365, around the time that The Worshipful Company of Plumbers was formed. In 1878, the City and Guilds of London Institute was formed by the City of London and 16 livery companies – the traditional guardians of work-based training – to develop a national system of technical education and qualifications.

Today, the majority of apprentices studying plumbing and heating attend their local Further Education College on a day-release basis. They can expect to take up to four years to gain their NVQ Level 3 Diploma.

The government may be keen to get youngsters into apprenticeship schemes now, but in the past apprentices were sadly neglected. In the 1960s/70s apprenticeship programmes began to decrease and less importance was placed on learning a trade. This resulted in a serious skills shortage in some industries, including plumbing and heating.

Back in 2004, the skills shortage really began to bite. Plumbers were in so much demand that college courses were over subscribed and many had long waiting lists for places. There were a few colleges that had around 2,000 people on a waiting list for a plumbing course!

Exaggerated media stories of high earnings brought an influx of people from other occupations into the industry. It wasn't unusual to find bank managers or IT specialists signing up at their local FE college to enrol on a plumbing course. The majority of these people didn't stay in the industry, mainly because they came in for the wrong reasons.

As we have already seen in chapter 2, you have to be a certain kind of person to do well in this trade. If you are keen to learn, like solving puzzles, enthusiastic and don't mind getting dirty, you are off to a good start!

There is no age limit for people attending plumbing courses, but there is on funding. If you are an apprentice aged between 16 and 24 there should be funding available to cover the cost. A section on financial help is included in chapter 11.

The following courses show some of the qualifications relating to plumbing and heating. This is not a complete list, as there are many courses on offer run by colleges and training centres that use different awarding bodies, such as BPEC or EAL; it's best to find out what is available in your area.

However, it must be stressed that only the NVQ Level 2/3 Diploma is the accepted industry standard at present for the skills necessary to become a professional plumber or heating and ventilating engineer. There has been much debate about raising the industry standard, in relation to qualifications, and it may be that in the future only the NVQ Level 3 Diploma (or equivalent) will be seen as acceptable. In Scotland this is already the case. Another important point is, these courses cannot be undertaken unless you are gaining work experience.

There's little doubt that the best route into the industry is via an apprenticeship scheme, where you are able to learn and earn at the same time. However, there are some courses that can be a good starting point. (*Information courtesy of City and Guilds.*)

Access to Building Services (2000)

This one year introductory qualification gives learners a flavour of the skills involved in four different areas of building services engineering; plumbing, electrotechnical, heating & ventilating and refrigeration & air conditioning.

Level 1 Diplomas in Plumbing/Electrical Installation (7202)

These qualifications are aimed at learners who want to learn the basic skills and knowledge of either plumbing or electrical installation.

Plumbing Craft (6035)

In this basic course you will learn how to deal with leaky pipes, water systems and drainage. These qualifications are intended for those wanting to gain the skills and knowledge necessary to enter the plumbing industry. At Level 2, this consists of a basic understanding, whilst the Level 3 Diploma equips learners with advanced plumbing knowledge and skills. This plumbing qualification will help you learn the trade and progress onto an NVQ course.

Heating and Ventilating (7188)

In this basic course, you will learn the theory and practical skills in order to work on industrial and commercial heating and ventilating systems. This qualification will help you learn the trade and progress on to an NVQ course.

NATIONAL VOCATIONAL QUALIFICATIONS

For England, Wales and Northern Ireland, the main plumbing qualifications are the National Vocational Qualifications (NVQs), or if you live in Scotland you will be entered for Scottish Vocational Qualifications (SVQs).

To gain entry on to these courses, you will probably find that most colleges are looking for students who have good GCSE grades in English, maths and science. However, requirements do vary, so it's a good idea to contact your nearest college to find out the qualifications needed to enrol on your chosen course.

It's quite likely that you will also be asked to do an assessment test and/or interview, before you are accepted on to the course. This will help the college to gauge your ability (see chapter 7 for sample questions). The reason for this is some students find they struggle with some elements of the course and drop out. The test may help to identify areas that you will need extra help, such as maths, or may show that you are not a suitable candidate.

The NVQ Level 2 Mechanical Engineering Services Plumbing course, requires students to have work experience in place. The reason for this is you will need to build a portfolio of work carried out on site, which will be assessed as part of the qualification. You can attend college on a block or day release basis.

Someone who has gained an NVQ Level 2 Diploma in Plumbing would most likely install simple cold water and hot water systems, carry out repairs to sanitary plumbing and drainage systems, and carry out repairs and simple modifications to wet central heating systems.

Those who have gained the NVQ Level 3 Diploma would be able to install more complex systems and would also be able to install heating systems, including domestic fuel burning appliances such as gas, oil or solid fuel boilers. They could also get involved with designing systems.

There are also NVQ qualifications available in Heating & Ventilating, Domestic Natural Gas Installation & Maintenance and Gas Network Operations, so it's best to talk to an advisor at the college to determine the right course for you.

However, it is worth mentioning that there are plans to make changes to courses relating to plumbing and domestic heating in 2017, when the new Trailblazer Apprenticeships are introduced.

For the time being, the following courses are aimed at NVQ Level 2/3 Diplomas:

Mechanical Engineering Services - Plumbing (Domestic) (C&G 6089)

This is for anyone wanting to become a qualified plumber. You must be working in a plumbing-related job to take the qualification. If you're just starting out in plumbing, you should take the Certificate in Plumbing Studies (6129) first, so you have the core knowledge you need.

Heating and Ventilating (C&G 6188)

On completion of the Level 2 & 3 NVQ Diplomas in Heating and Ventilation, the learner will be in possession of the practical skills and knowledge to work on a range of specialised industrial, commercial and domestic installations.

Plumbing and Domestic Heating (C&G 6189)

These qualifications cover all the essential knowledge and skills needed for a successful career in domestic plumbing and heating. The Level 2 qualification is designed especially for new entrants to the industry, providing them with the basic skills and experience they need. The Level 3 qualification is aimed at those who have already completed the Level 2 qualification, or with some relevant experience and knowledge of the industry. Those choosing gas-related units at Level 3, will achieve the Gas Safe licence to practise on successful completion of the qualification.

Note: Anyone who has an old Technical Certificate in Plumbing or H&V, can still use these to 'upgrade' their qualification to an NVQ and complete the on site elements of the 6189 and 6188 respectively, as there are pathways to enable this to happen.

T LEVEL QUALIFICATIONS

'T Levels' are new technical study programmes being developed that will sit alongside apprenticeships within a reformed skills training system. Construction will be in the first wave of subjects available in September 2020, with the full set of T Levels introduced by 2022.

This technical option will prepare individuals for skilled employment, which requires technical knowledge and practical skills valued by industry. T Levels will be for students aged between 16-19-years-old who want to develop work-related knowledge and skills, but are not yet clear about the specific occupation they want to work in.

PROFESSIONAL QUALIFICATIONS

Professional qualifications are important in the industry as they will increase your earning potential, improve your career prospects and will raise your professional credibility. Once you are fully qualified and have gained experience, you might want to consider applying for a professional qualification such as Engineering Technician, Incorporated Engineer or Chartered Engineer. This is achieved by registration with the Engineering Council. Entry must be via membership of a *professional engineering institution.

EngTech

The Engineering Technician (EngTech) professional registration is open to anyone who can demonstrate the required professional competences and commitment. Typically, applicants will have successfully completed an Advanced/Modern Apprenticeship or other work-based learning programme.

What are the benefits?

• Recognition of your expertise and hard work • Self-esteem • Higher earning potential • Improved career prospects • Greater influence within your organisation and industry • Access to life-long learning resources • Letters after your name, e.g. J.Smith EngTech.

IEng

Professional registration as an Incorporated Engineer (IEng) recognises your proven competence, commitment, skills and experience. It is an important milestone in the career of any engineer or technologist. In particular, IEng registration shows your employer and peers that you have demonstrated a commitment to professional standards, and to developing and enhancing your competence.

What are the benefits?

• Recognition that you are a professional • Identifying that you have the competences, expertise and work ethics that employers value • High status and self-esteem • Improved career prospects • Greater influence within your organisation and industry • Higher earnings potential • Access to life-long learning • Being part of a network of professional engineers • International recognition of your professional qualification • Demonstration that your competence may be compared with standards applicable in other parts of the world • Letters after your name e.g. J.Smith IEng.

CEng

The Chartered Engineer (CEng) professional registration is open to anyone who can demonstrate the required professional competences and commitment – usually at degree level. These are set out in the Engineering Council's professional standard, UK-SPEC.

What are the benefits?

Similar to IEng status. You would also be seen as being part of a technological elite and would have letters after your name e.g. J.Smith CEng.

* Professional Engineering Institutions include: Chartered Institution of Building Services Engineers (CIBSE), Chartered Institute of Plumbing & Heating Engineering (CIPHE), Chartered Institution of Water and Environmental Management (CIWEM), Institute of Water, Institution of Gas Engineers and Managers (IGEM).

Further information is available from the Engineering Council.

CHAPTER 9
PROGRESSION

If you thought opportunities for progression in the plumbing and heating industry were limited, you couldn't be more wrong! With hard work and determination there are many avenues open to you, as you will see from the case studies. However, you may need to gain extra qualifications for certain roles.

Now we are going to look at the main roles in more detail and also give an idea of where they might lead in terms of developing your career. If you study and put in the effort, you will find a career in the plumbing and heating industry that is satisfying to do, as well as being financially rewarding.

DOMESTIC PLUMBER

A typical domestic plumber will carry out a wide range of work, according to the qualifications and experience they have gained. This will include installing baths, showers, toilets, bidets and wash basins; hot and cold water systems; a wide range of heating systems, including appliances fuelled by gas, coal, oil and wood; above and below ground drainage systems. They will also carry out maintenance and repair work, including servicing boilers.

Further training and qualifications could result in a domestic plumber installing solar thermal and solar photovoltaic (PV) panel systems; biomass heating systems, air source and ground source heat pumps; grey water recycling systems and rainwater harvesting systems.

Career Opportunities

There is usually a steady flow of work for domestic plumbers. Once you have gained your qualifications and enough experience in the industry, you may find you want new challenges, or just want to change direction.

Your Own Business: This will take a lot of hard work to get established, but you would be your own boss. This should never be considered an easy option though as it will take some time to build up a business. There are a lot of financial outlays involved in being self-employed; you might need to hire business premises or buy a van or expensive tools. On top of that you will also have to pay for professional indemnity insurance to protect yourself and your customers. Remember, if you work for yourself you will not get sick pay or paid holidays. It's likely that you will also have to pay an accountant to keep your books in order.

Technical Representative: If you want to come off the 'tools' there are lots of other options open to you. With the experience you have gained you could do well in many areas associated with the industry, such as working as a technical representative for a manufacturer of plumbing and heating products. In that role you would assist designers and buyers and visit sites to advise installers on the best way to tackle the installation of their products.

Technical Helpline: Alternatively, you could work on a technical helpline where you would advise buyers, installers and members of the public on manufacturers' products and answer queries about installation and suitability of products for particular applications.

Sales: Plumbing merchants need staff who understand the practical side of the work to advise customers on the best products, appliances and tools for the job.

Plumbing Lecturer: Once you have gained an NVQ Level 3 Diploma in plumbing, your prospects will increase. If you are happy to study further and would like to pass on your skills, you could train to become a plumbing lecturer – this would mean gaining a teaching qualification.

Trainer: Lots of plumbing and heating manufacturers have facilities to train installers. This ensures that products and materials are correctly installed, serviced and repaired. You could also be involved in teaching CPD courses.

Inspector: Water companies employ Water Regulations Inspectors to ensure that the design and installation of plumbing systems, water fittings and water-using appliances, comply to national requirements and do not contaminate or disrupt the water supply in their area. Inspections are carried out on domestic and non-domestic premises.

Expert Witness: An expert witness is acknowledged as having the right skills, training, qualifications and experience to give a professional opinion in the case of a dispute – either in workmanship or materials used. Sometimes you would need to attend court to give evidence. Normally, you would need to be registered with the Engineering Council to carry out Expert Witness work.

Further progression

Gain a degree: You could also consider studying for an engineering degree. This could lead to working as a consultant or public health engineer (a designer of water supply and drainage systems).

COMMERCIAL/INDUSTRIAL PLUMBER

An NVQ Level 3 is the preferred qualification to work in the industrial or commercial sector. A lot of the work is similar to that carried out by a domestic plumber, but it is often more complex and on a larger scale. For instance, you could be part of a team refurbishing bathrooms in a hotel or installing a wide range of commercial or industrial heating systems.

You could also be involved in installing automatic sprinklers and other fire protection systems, drainage systems involving acid nuetralisation or oil and grease removal and mechanical ventilation systems.

Commercial or industrial plumbers who gain additional qualifications would also be able to work on rainwater harvesting systems, grey water recycling systems and renewable energy technologies, such as solar thermal systems and PV panel systems.

Career Opportunities

Besides the opportunities listed for a domestic plumber, you may find other opportunities open to you. For instance, if you work for a sizeable plumbing or construction company and show initiative, you could go on to become an estimator, buyer, chargehand or project engineer.

Estimator: You will need to be good at accurately calculating the amount of materials that will be needed for a particular job. You will also have to work out how many people will need to be involved and how much time it will take to complete the project.

Buyer: You will need to know where to get the best deal in respect of price and quality, when it comes to selecting products and materials for the job being undertaken. This will involve negotiating with manufacturers and merchants to get the best price.

Chargehand: You will need to be able to supervise the plumbers working on the job and deal with any problems that arise. This will involve good communication skills and ideally an authoritative manner.

Project Engineer: With enough experience, you could become a project engineer. This entails being capable of running a number of projects at the same time, dealing with any problems and making sure costs don't escalate.

Management: There are advantages in working for a big company, because in time it may be possible for you to rise in the ranks and eventually become a manager or director – who knows, one day you could be the CEO!

Design Engineer: With the right training you could consider specialising in a certain area, such as designing and installing vacuum drainage systems (systems not restricted by the use of gravity fed plumbing) and syphonic rainwater systems (this is when water is syphoned from the roof down into the drain at high velocity).

H&V Engineer: Plumbers in the commercial/industrial sector often specialise in areas such as heating and ventilating. H&V engineers install and commission complex heating and ventilating systems in large buildings.

Further progression

Gain a degree: Gaining a degree would open a lot of doors for you. For instance you could progress further and could become a heating and ventilating design engineer or a public health engineer.

GAS FITTER

To legally install or service any gas appliances you will need to have an ACS (Accredited Certification Scheme) qualification and be registered with Gas Safe. Gas service technicians install, service and repair gas appliances and heating systems. These include gas fires, boilers, water heaters and cookers. You might also work on appliances that use Liquefied Petroleum Gas (LPG).

Career Opportunities

If you just have an ACS qualification, you could think about training to gain plumbing qualifications, as this would lead to more work opportunities (see information on domestic plumber). Manufacturers of gas boilers run training centres for installers, so there may be openings for instructors.

After you have gained experience in the industry, there may be opportunities to pass on your skills to others by becoming an ACS tutor/assessor.

You could work as a self-employed gas technician. If you have an NVQ Level 3 qualification, you could undergo further training to design complex gas delivery systems, or assess energy efficiency in large-scale commercial developments.

LEADWORKER

Up until a few years ago, leadwork was part of the curriculum in NVQ plumbing courses. This is not the case nowadays. However, for those people who have undergone training in leadwork, there are opportunities to use your skills.

There is a demand for specialist sheet metal workers, who are able to carry out work on historical and commercial buildings using copper, zinc or lead.

Career Opportunities

Companies carrying out restoration work to listed historical buildings, such as castles and churches, employ specialist leadworkers. Sometimes this is done on a contract basis, so if you are self-employed you could find your services in demand. This would normally include: flashings around chimneys and joints: ornamental work, such as domes, turrets and spires; cladding and dormers. It's interesting work and you could be involved in projects concerning famous buildings, such as the Tower of London or Windsor Castle.

CLIMBING THE LADDER

Joining a professional body

There are a number of professional bodies you can join, which will raise your status in the industry (see list in the contacts section). However, the Chartered Institute of Plumbing and Heating Engineering (CIPHE) is the only body that offers individual professional recognition for your plumbing and heating qualifications and experience.

There are a number of categories for membership, starting at Trainee level and progressing up to Fellow. The CIPHE supports members with CPD activities and has an online e-learning portal. Besides that, there are many advantages associated with membership, including discounts on insurance and other services, which will help you to recover the cost of your membership fee.

CHAPTER 10
CASE STUDIES

Case Study Five:

Ben Bowers (27) thought it would be a good idea to train for a trade, so he could gain a worthwhile qualification. He admits he was very lucky in the way he met his employer.

"A local engineer was working across the road from where I live and my dad asked him if he needed any help – he said 'yes'. I spent the next four and a half years working for him, full-time. I attended Gloucestershire College as an apprentice and gained an NVQ Level 3 Heating qualification."

Ben finished his apprenticeship in 2009 and in 2010 started up on his own as BB Plumbing and Heating. In 2012 he entered a partnership, which helped to grow the business. The partnership ended at the beginning of 2015 and Ben Bowers Heating Solutions Ltd was formed in the January.

His company carries out a wide range of plumbing and heating work, from bathrooms to bespoke heating systems. Primarily they carry out installation and maintenance on many heating systems from gas and oil to biomass. They offer individually designed heating systems to suit individual needs and requirements.

"During my apprenticeship we carried out many jobs within the solid fuel industry, from installing wood burners to installing back boilers to link into existing heating systems. As soon as I went on my own I gained the HETAS qualification for stove installation, both wet and dry, so I could continue doing this type of work. I decided that biomass was the natural progression from normal solid fuel boilers/stoves, so decided to gain qualifications in this field."

The next step for Ben was to become MCS accredited (Microgeneration Certification Scheme). When he originally looked at the requirements it all seemed a bit too much, but he persevered and gained his qualification through HETAS.

"They were very quick and efficient in helping me gain accreditation. I had to find a job where they would allow me to install a biomass boiler on the understanding I would use it for my accreditation. Luckily, an opportunity arose quite quickly and I fitted my first biomass boiler, which HETAS inspected as part of the approval process.

"Finally they carried out an office audit to ensure I was running my business to MCS standard. For a company of my size the office audit was the most difficult part, as I was trying to juggle doing all the physical installation work whilst doing all the paperwork. I now employ somebody to assist with admin, which has helped hugely."

Ben believes there is a rapidly growing demand for renewable energy and this is amplified with the Renewable Heat Incentive (RHI).

"People are becoming very conscious of how they heat their homes and spend their money, so if they can install environmentally friendly systems with the benefit of gaining cash incentives, then I can only see the market growing. Once the RHI dwindles out, who knows what will happen."

Ben has the following advice for people coming into the industry:

"Gain the correct qualifications and experience rather than doing a fast-track course. Every site is different and no one can demonstrate this in a short period of time. I think an apprenticeship is the best way to gain the correct experience and qualifications.

"Once qualified, stick to doing high standard work rather than rushing jobs for a quick buck. Word of mouth is the best form of advertising for us, so every customer is as important as the next. A good reputation can take years to gain but seconds to destroy, so quality is the key."

As for the future, Ben is hoping to open a HETAS approved showroom demonstrating some of the products they offer, along with continuing to build his business to a high standard.

"I already have one engineer who did his apprenticeship with me and last year I took on another 16-year-old apprentice, with the aim of long-term employment. Hopefully, we can grow steadily over the coming years giving the right people the opportunity to learn within the industry. Even though it's my business, we all get on brilliantly and nobody is treated better or worse than the other – 'team-work makes the dream work!'"

Case Study Six:

Danny Davis has been in the plumbing and heating industry for around 18 years. He started off his career by working for his father, who runs a plumbing and heating business in Manchester.

Danny was interested in plumbing at an early age and as he got older he helped out in the school holidays and weekends. However, he wasn't sure he wanted a career in plumbing, so he decided to go to college to take A-Levels. It was at this time that Danny suffered a brain haemorrhage.

"I was an amateur boxer and took a blow to the head, which resulted in a number of operations to repair the damage. I was 18 at the time. As part of my rehabilitation I started working for my father. It wasn't long before I decided that I wanted to be a professional plumber."

Danny enrolled on an NVQ Level 2 course in Mechanical Engineering Services Plumbing, on a day release basis. He went on to gain his NVQ Level 3 and several other qualifications, covering Water Regulations and solar thermal installations.

One day, Danny was reading a trade magazine when he saw an article about a new award for young plumbers committed to career and skills development. He decided to enter and became the first recipient of the Raymond J Brooks Scholarship.

"I couldn't believe it when I won. The scholarship provided me with the opportunity to travel to the USA where I was able to travel around many different states, studying their approach to training and development. I got a really good insight into how the American plumbing and heating industry operates. I met some wonderful people too, it was a truly fantastic experience!"

After completing his four-year apprenticeship, Danny applied for a job as a technical officer at the Chartered Institute of Plumbing and Heating Engineering (CIPHE), based in Hornchurch, Essex. By that time he'd gained nearly seven years' experience working with his father, first on a part-time basis and then full-time. Besides the experience Danny had gained in the day-to-day work as a plumbing and heating engineer, he had also been actively involved in CPD, attending various technical training courses, seminars and exhibitions. He got the job.

"I have to admit, it was a big step starting a new career hundreds of miles away from my family. But I soon made friends and settled into my new life."

Since then, Danny has been progressing up the career ladder. In 2008 he was promoted to senior technical officer and in 2012 he was promoted once again to operations manager. It's a demanding role where he has to oversee many projects.

"In some respects I do miss working on the tools. I got a lot of satisfaction at the end of the day when I looked at the work I'd done. Don't get me wrong, I still find my work interesting and satisfying, but working in a predominantly office-based environment is very different to working 'on site'. I now have longer term goals, which depend on the teamwork of others."

Danny's working day starts at 9am and finishes around 5pm, but he often finds himself in the office a lot longer than that. He is also expected to attend events and meetings out of hours, sometimes on weekends. On some occasions he may have to travel abroad to meetings, so may be away from home for a few days at a time.

Danny has the following advice to anyone thinking of a career in the plumbing and heating industry.

"I'm glad I chose a career in plumbing and would recommend it to others. It doesn't matter if you are on the tools or have taken another career route in the industry; you need to take every opportunity to develop your skills as you go along. I am still attending courses and seminars – life-long learning is the key to success!"

CHAPTER 11
FUNDING, AWARDS and COMPETITIONS

Most youngsters who gain a plumbing apprenticeship will not have to worry about course fees, etc. However, they may need some financial help in other areas. This is particularly relevant to mature students who are changing careers. The following organisations may be able to help...

BPEC Charity

The BPEC Support Fund offers training grants of up to £2,500 and is designed to help raise skill levels in plumbing and heating, or to help charitable projects to be completed. It's aimed at individuals who either work in the plumbing and heating industries and wish to improve their skills and knowledge, or to those working towards the next level of qualifications. It also applies to those who wish to enter the industry for the first time.

How do I apply?

Applicants can download an application form, or complete it on-line at **www.bpec.org.uk**

City & Guilds

City & Guilds offer a small number of bursaries (educational grants) each year to people who would like the opportunity to study for a City & Guilds qualification and who would otherwise be financially unable to study.

The bursaries can be used for a wide range of purposes including:

• Paying your course and/or exam fees • Covering living costs if you are unable to work while you study • Covering childcare or travel expenses • Covering other costs that are making it difficult for you to enrol on a course.

How do I apply?

Applicants must be aged 16 or over. Further information is available at **www.cityandguilds.com**

Family Action

This organisation offers small educational grants in the region of £200 to a maximum of £300. The grants are to cover additional costs associated with a course of study such as clothing and/or equipment required for the course, travel, examination costs, computers/laptops. They are aimed at individuals over 14 years of age.

How do I apply?

Applications must be submitted on-line, by authorised members of college staff (usually student welfare advisors or equivalent) from affiliated organisations. Find out more from **www.family-action.org.uk**

Family Cash

This website has a wealth of information on financial help for individuals and families. It has a section on financial assistance for educational needs, as well as educational loans for over 24s.

How do I apply?

You'll find all the information you need on their website **www.familycash.org.uk**

Prince's Trust

The Prince's Trust offers development awards to help tackle financial barriers that may prevent individuals from accessing education, training or employment. The grant can be used for a wide range of purposes including:

• Tools or equipment for a job or qualification e.g. hairdressing kit, plumbing tools, chef's whites • Course fees • Interview clothes • License fees e.g. CSCS card (construction) • Childcare costs to help single parents access short-term education • Transport to a new job until first pay cheque.

Applications will be assessed based on availability of local funding, which varies across the country. If you are eligible for a development award and funding is available in your local area, you will be invited to an assessment meeting before submitting your application for final decision. The whole process can take up to six weeks, so applications should be made well in advance, if possible.

How do I apply?

Initially, individuals have to answer questions such as:

• What do you need the funding for? • How much money do you need? • Have you looked into other possible sources of funding? • Will the funding help you into education, training or work?

There is an on-line enquiry form at **www.princes-trust.org.uk**

The Worshipful Company of Plumbers

The Worshipful Company of Plumbers (WCP), considers bursaries of up to £1,000 for students who have successfully completed their NVQ Level 2 Diploma in Mechanical Engineering Services (MES) and are enrolled on the Level 3 MES Plumbing course.

Representatives of the Company's Technical Committee will interview candidates who will be required to demonstrate how the bursary is to be spent to assist their course studies e.g. cost of text books, tools and travelling expenses.

How do I apply?

The Company invites professional bodies, training providers or employers to nominate students who, in their opinion, meet the criteria and would therefore merit consideration as possible recipients of a bursary. However, applications from individual students are also welcome.

You can download an application form from the WCP website – **www.plumberscompany.org.uk**

AWARDS

In this section we are going to look at some of the special awards that may be obtained throughout different stages of your career in the plumbing and heating industry. Besides the prestige gained from achieving an award, it can help with career progression – a brilliant addition to your CV!

CIPHE

The Chartered Institute of Plumbing and Heating Engineering acts as the secretariat for three awards that are available to members. These awards were introduced jointly by The Worshipful Company of Plumbers, CIPHE and City & Guilds in 2001. Many other trades now use this Certificate scheme to produce their own awards.

- Apprentice Plumber Certificate
- Journeyman Plumber Certificate
- Master Plumber Certificate

Apprentice Certificate: This is an award for people who qualify by study, training, assessment or examination at NVQ Level 2 (or equivalent), with the necessary work experience. Successful applicants also commit themselves to proceed to NVQ Level 3.

Journeyman Certificate: Applicants for this award will have achieved success at NVQ Level 3 (or equivalent) and will be setting out to accumulate further experience. This will include supplementary qualifications and demonstrating an active interest in upholding professional standards.

Master Certificate: Any Member (MCIPHE) or Fellow (FCIPHE) of the CIPHE can apply for the Master Plumber Certificate, provided they are qualified to NVQ Level 3 and have adequate experience in plumbing. In addition, successful candidates must submit evidence of CPD when providing their CV. They also have to be registered as either an Engineering Technician, Incorporated or Chartered Engineer with the Engineering Council.

How do I apply?

Application forms and further information can be downloaded from the CIPHE website **www.ciphe.org.uk**

The Worshipful Company of Plumbers

The WCP has supported the development of the profession for centuries and this objective is just as relevant today. The Company offers a variety of awards to recognise exceptional work in plumbing. The Company awards include the following:

Gold Medal: For students who have achieved the highest standard in NVQ Level 3 Certificate in MES (Plumbing).

Silver Medal: For students who have achieved the highest standard in NVQ Level 2 Certificate in MES (Plumbing).

Plumbing Teacher Award: For colleges that teach the winning student in each of the National Plumbing Competition elements of the National SkillBuild Competition.

Leonard Hearsey Award: For volunteer demonstrators at the Company's museum and workshop at the Weald and Downland Museum at Singleton, West Sussex.

How do I apply?

Application forms and further information can be downloaded from the WCP website. Search 'Awards' **www.plumberscompany.org.uk**

J B Wilkinson Merit Shield: Colleges in the northern counties are eligible to enter plumbing students for the award. It's for students who have achieved the highest standard in NVQ Level 2 Certificate in MES (Plumbing). The award is administered by the Newcastle Branch of the CIPHE.

How do I apply?

You will find information on these awards on the WCP website **www.plumberscompany.org.uk** along with contact details.

SKILLS COMPETITIONS

Skills competitions are also worth a mention because if you take part, it will show your employer (or prospective employer) that you are keen to improve yourself. It doesn't matter if you win or not (although, it is a bonus to come first!), it will look good on your CV.

In a skills competition, students have to follow detailed plans and complete the task within a certain time frame. This helps to build confidence in their abilities.

There are national skills competitions aimed at plumbing apprentices; usually contestants take part in regional competitions first and the winners go on to the final. These competitions will usually be advertised throughout the colleges. Some colleges partner with other organisations, such as the CIPHE and the WCP and run a competition just for its own students.

SkillPLUMB

SkillPLUMB is a national plumbing competition run by BPEC. Regional heats around the UK are staged in the early part of the year. The highest scoring competitors are then invited to compete at the UK final, which is usually held in November at The Skills Show at the NEC, Birmingham – the largest skills and careers show in the UK.

All finalists receive prizes including tools, workwear and vouchers alongside a competition medallion and certificate.

High scoring competitors may also be eligible for a place at the prestigious WorldSkills competition, which is run every other year in countries around the world.

HIP UK Heating Apprentice of the Year

The HIP UK Heating Apprentice of the Year competition was launched in 2008 by SNG Publishing Ltd (publishers of the *HIP Magazine* aimed at plumbing students). There are six regional heats, in the early part of the year, and the final usually takes place around the end of April.

The finalists all receive a special cut glass trophy, a certificate of achievement and a range of tools. The outright winner usually comes away with prizes amounting to £2,500.

In 2018, the prizes up for grabs were worth a staggering £9,000 from the competition's sponsors!

CHAPTER 12
CASE STUDY

Case Study Seven:

After leaving school with O-Level qualifications back in 1987, Chris Northey was unsure what he wanted to do. His father suggested that he help him in his plumbing and heating business in the summer holidays. He soon became very interested in the work and enjoyed learning about the types of tools and materials that were used in the job. It was at this point that he decided he wanted to do this for a living.

Chris started his career by studying for the City & Guilds Craft and Advanced Craft Certificate in Plumbing. During his six years working in the family business he developed many new skills and interests, right from the design through to the actual installation of the plumbing and heating systems within a building. He also gained skills associated with the servicing of gas and oil fired boilers for hot water and central heating systems. As part of the job, Chris had the task of estimating materials and the time it would take to carry out the work.

"I wanted to learn as much as possible about the design side of plumbing and heating systems. I felt that it was very important to understand why systems were installed the way they were and the technical side of the design process was an important aspect for me at that time."

Chris then went on to gain the BTEC Ordinary and Higher National Certificate in Building Studies. Following on from this, he spent three years at Reading University, where he studied for and gained a BEng (Hons) Building Services Engineering Design & Management degree.

Chris Northey now works as head of public health engineering for BDSP Partnership (consulting engineers), based in London. He has had a number of high profile jobs.

He is responsible for managing a team of public health engineers, but his main duties include undertaking and overseeing all aspects of public health engineering services design, from concept through to project handover.

"A public health design engineer can just about get involved in the design of every type of building you can think of during their career, from schools, hospitals, laboratories, shops, offices, hotels, leisure facilities, stadiums, museums, libraries and domestic properties – the list is endless.

"The jobs can also vary in size, complexity and location, both within the UK and the rest of the world. Clean drinking water supplies and adequate sanitary/drainage systems are the most important basic provisions we all need, to ensure human health and wellbeing. Public health engineering affects us all!"

As far as job satisfaction goes, Chris couldn't be happier.

"I totally enjoy and am completely satisfied in my every day work as a public health design engineer. I am constantly challenged to produce high quality designs for many projects and remain motivated to produce the best solution every time. My job satisfaction is also enhanced with the wide number and type of jobs that I work on at any one time."

However, this is a demanding role and Chris has many responsibilities. Besides producing his own engineering work he also oversees the work of other members within his team. This means that he often works between 50-60 hours per week. Chris doesn't find it a problem, as he knows that the way to reach the top of his profession is through sheer hard work.

A number of the projects that Chris has been involved with span over several years, so he gets satisfaction seeing how everything develops and comes together. He also gets to meet many other highly skilled and experienced engineers and personnel on a daily basis.

Chris is keen to encourage youngsters to consider a career in the plumbing and heating industry and is also involved with training.

"I really enjoy passing on my skills to others and I do my best to promote public health engineering as a career to those already in the industry and to apprentices. There's a full career path now, which leads from plumbing apprentice to Chartered Engineer. If you are interested in design, like to solve problems and have drive and enthusiasm – this could be the career choice for you."

Chris has received a number of industry awards, which include the 1991 Lilli Sarah Barber Memorial Gold Medal from The Worshipful Company of Plumbers. Chris was also awarded the IIE's Career Achievement Award for 2004, for demonstrating exceptional commitment to engineering through his academic and professional development. In 2011 he was awarded the City & Guilds Prince Philip Medal for his outstanding leadership, ability and enthusiasm he has shown throughout his career in the engineering industry. In 2015, Chris received the CIBSE Silver Medal Award for his outstanding service to the Institution.

CHAPTER 13
IS IT FOR YOU?

After reading this book you may still have a few questions. In this chapter you will find a section on frequently asked questions, followed by pros and cons of training to become a plumber. Good luck in your future career, whatever it may be!

Q – I trained as a plasterer, but want to change careers and become a plumber. I'm 35, am I too old?

A – No, you are not too old, but you will have to pay your own course fees. It is possible that because you already have a useful skill it might be a bit easier to find someone to give you work experience. Also, if you can still earn some money as a plasterer while you are studying, it will be a big help. It is an advantage to be multi-skilled in the job market.

Q – I've seen a few adverts offering distance-learning courses in plumbing. This looks like a good option as I wouldn't have to quit my job, but would this lead to a recognised plumbing qualification?

A – This would not be a good idea. You need an adequate amount of practical study and work experience to back up the theoretical side. You would not be able to gain an NVQ Level 2/3 Diploma this way.

Q – I want to apply for an apprenticeship in plumbing, but I know I'm going to get a low grade in my English GCSE...

A – Most plumbing departments in colleges are looking for students who have obtained at least four A-C passes, which usually includes English and maths, but this does vary. However, if they think you have potential they will be able to offer extra tuition to help raise your level of English (or maths), so get in touch with them for a chat.

Q – Someone has offered me work experience, but they say I won't be paid – can they do that?

A – Yes, they can. Usually you'll find that sole-traders might be interested in getting some help, but are not able to pay a wage. It's up to you to decide if you accept their offer. If you prove your worth, you may find you get offered paid work at a later stage.

Q – I recently began an apprenticeship with a small plumbing company. I like the people I work with, but most of my day is spent carrying tools/materials, making cups of tea and clearing up after jobs. I thought I would be doing more plumbing.

A – Don't worry, the job may feel restricted at the moment, but it's all part of learning the trade. Watch carefully how jobs are carried out and be keen to help. Before you know it you will be fully involved.

Q – I have to do an assessment test at my local college, to see if I am suitable to join the plumbing course. How difficult will it be?

A – Like all tests, the better you are prepared, the easier it will be. These tests usually cover literacy skills, numerical skills and applied science and mathematical aptitude (see chapter 7 for sample questions). To help you prepare, you could pop along to your local library and ask the librarian to recommend some books to you.

Q – I've written to a dozen plumbing companies asking for an apprenticeship, but I haven't had a reply from any of them.

A – Did you remember to include a stamped, self-addressed envelope? Sometimes it's better to print off copies of your CV and take it to the plumbing company personally. Remember to look smart and be as enthusiastic as you can. If they say they are not interested in taking anyone on at the moment, ask if they could keep your details on file, just in case...

Q – I've just got my GCSE results and haven't worked at all, so why do I need a CV?

A – You may not have worked before but you can add other information that shows you could be a good candidate. Besides listing your GCSE grades, you could list hobbies and interests that show you have skills. See chapter 3 for tips on writing a CV.

Q – I've been offered an interview to become an apprentice with a local plumbing company. What type of questions will they ask me?

A – Typical questions would be: Why do you want to work here? What do you know about our company? What can you do for us that someone else can't?

What the interviewer really wants to know is: Do you know what we do? Why have you chosen to apply to this company?

When talking about why you want to work for the employer, focus on what you can do for them, not on what they can do for you. Be honest and enthusiastic.

It's a good idea to pop to your library to look for a book on interview techniques. It will boost your confidence if you are well prepared.

Q – I have dyslexia, can I still train to be a plumber?

A – This condition should not stop you from training to be a plumber. Dyslexics often excel at solving puzzles – one of the traits that is a mark of a good plumber. The college should have a learning support department, which will give you all the help you need. Remember to tell the college you have dyslexia right from the beginning, it won't go against you, in fact they will give you extra time if you have to take an entrance exam or assessment.

PROS AND CONS

Here are some other things to consider before making up your mind.

ADVANTAGES

In demand

Professional plumbers are always in demand, so it's a job with a future. There is a wide range of qualifications available to help you progress in your career. On top of that you can gain membership of professional bodies to help you climb the ladder.

Variety

There is a huge amount of variety in the work that plumbers do, so you won't get bored! You are also likely to get job satisfaction through seeing projects through from start to finish.

Start your own business

Once you have gained your qualifications and have enough experience in the industry, you could consider starting up your own business. However, this is quite a big step and you will need to give it a lot of careful consideration.

Diversity

Women can earn a good living from working as a plumber and if they are self-employed and have a family, they can choose the hours they want to work.

Money

You can earn a good wage as a professional plumber or heating installer. Some plumbing companies offer an out of hours emergency service, which enables plumbers to earn a higher income. The downside is work is likely disrupt your evenings and weekends, which could make things difficult for your social life.

DISADVANTAGES

Perception

Public perception of plumbers can be negative. Unfortunately, there are a lot of people calling themselves plumbers who do not have the right qualifications (if any at all), or experience to do a good job. When cases of bad plumbing practice appear as news stories, the public becomes wary of plumbers generally. Although these 'cowboys' are in the minority, other plumbers become tainted. On the plus side, if you carry out a good job at a reasonable price, it's likely your customer will recommend you to family and friends and you will gain a good reputation.

Working with the public

As with any job that you have face-to-face contact with the public, there can be conflict. Usually arguments will develop if the customer feels they are being taken advantage of. Unfortunately, no two installations are the same and sometimes you may find yourself in a situation where you need extra materials and time to finish the job. Avoid upsetting the customer by fully explaining the situation. Good communication is vital to resolving problems amicably.

Dirty work

The very nature of the job can result in plumbers being involved in smelly and dirty work. That includes coming into contact with raw sewage. This is not a job for the faint-hearted!

Head for heights

You may be involved in installations where you need to climb a ladder or work from a scaffold. If you have a fear of heights, this could be a problem.

Risks to health

Plumbers, along with other tradespeople, face health risks that could lead to serious illness. A good example of this is inhaling asbestos dust. Asbestos is found in thousands of buildings built before the year 2000. It does not present a health risk if it is undisturbed, but if material containing asbestos is chipped, drilled, broken or allowed to deteriorate, it can release a fine dust that contains asbestos fibres. When the dust is breathed in, the asbestos fibres enter the lungs and can gradually damage them over time. This can result in a form of lung cancer or scarring of the lung tissue.

The key to keeping safe is to wear protective clothing, helmets, masks, goggles, or other garments or equipment designed to protect the wearer's body from injury or infection.

Damage to joints

Plumbers who have been in the trade a long time often end up with joint or spinal problems. However, a lot of this damage would have been caused through not correctly lifting heavy objects. A lot of kneeling can also cause problems, especially in later life. Wearing adequate protection, such as kneepads will help you to avoid injury.

CHAPTER 14
CONTACTS

EDUCATION AND TRAINING

APPRENTICESHIPS – www.apprenticeships.org.uk

This site gives lots of information on apprenticeships and traineeships. It also has a list of vacancies and tips on writing an application for an apprenticeship.

BESA – www.thebesa.com
Email: enquiries@thebesa.com – Tel: 020 7313 4900

Building Engineering Services Association (BESA) is involved with apprenticeship training for a number of sectors in the building industry.

BPEC – www.bpec.org.uk/training
Email: info@bpec.org.uk – Tel: 0845 644 6558

BPEC works closely with a nationwide network of employers, colleges and private training providers to enable them to offer a range of quality training materials, assessments and qualifications. BPEC also organises the SkillPLUMB national skills competition.

BRITISH GAS – www.britishgasacademy.co.uk

You will find information on British Gas apprenticeships and traineeships along with current positions they want to fill.

CITY & GUILDS – www.cityandguilds.com
Tel: 0844 543 0033

You will be able to find details on City & Guilds qualifications available for the plumbing and heating industry. You can also use this site to find a City & Guilds approved training centre.

CONNEXIONS – www.connexions-tw.co.uk

This is a good place to chat to a careers advisor if you live in the north of England – specifically Gateshead, Newcastle, North Tyneside, South Tyneside and Sunderland.

EAL – www.eal.org.uk
E-mail: customercare@eal.org.uk – Tel: 01923 652400

EAL is an awarding body for engineering, technology and related sectors, offering a wide range of vocational qualifications for the industry.

HETAS – www.hetas.co.uk
Email: info@hetas.co.uk – Tel: 01684 278170

HETAS is the leading training provider for solid fuel, wood and biomass, offering comprehensive courses specifically designed for installers, retailers and specifiers,

INSTITUTE FOR APPRENTICESHIPS –
www.instituteforapprenticeships.org
Email: enquiries.ifa@education.gov.uk

Their remit is to ensure the development of high-quality apprenticeships so they are viewed and respected as highly as other education routes.

JTL – www.jtltraining.com
Talk to an advisor on 0800 0852 308

JTL is a not-for-profit charity, offering advanced apprenticeships in plumbing, heating & ventilating and engineering maintenance. They also provide a wide range of professional development courses.

LEARNDIRECT – www.learndirect.co.uk
Tel: 0800 101 901

This site gives information on courses that you might find helpful if you want to improve your communications skills, literacy and numeracy. A number of these are free (including English and maths).

LONDON APPRENTICESHIP COMPANY – www.londonapprenticeship.co.uk
Email: info@londonapprenticeship.co.uk
Tel: 020 3651 4747

If you live in the London area it's worth visiting this site. There is an on-line application process for apprenticeships.

NATIONAL CAREERS SERVICE – https://nationalcareersservice.direct.gov. uk
Contact an advisor on 0800 100 900

Another useful website, which not only gives careers information, but also offers advice on interview techniques and gives tips on creating CVs.

GAS SAFETY

GAS SAFE – www.gassaferegister.co.uk
Tel: 0800 408 5500

It is against the law for anyone to work on gas appliances in the United Kingdom, Isle of Man or Guernsey unless they are Gas Safe registered.

GOVERNMENT WEBSITES

DIRECTGOV – www.direct.gov.uk

Visit the education and learning section to find information about accessing student loans, bursaries and grants.

HEALTH & SAFETY EXECUTIVE (HSE) – www.hse.gov.uk

This is the place to visit if you have any concerns on health or safety. You'll find information on risks at work, including working with asbestos and how to prevent damage to your joints when lifting heavy weights.

ORGANISATIONS FOR WOMEN

FEMALE PLUMBER NETWORK – Twitter: @she-plumbs

Non-profit network for female plumbers in the UK, offering mutual support & advice, sharing business ideas and training.

WISE – www.wisecampaign.org.uk
Tel: 0113 222 6072

Women into Science and Engineering (WISE) is another useful site that encourages girls to think about a career in the science or engineering sector. You can subscribe to their newsletter and/or get a free weekly job alert of all the latest job vacancies listed on the WISE website.

WOMEN INSTALLERS TOGETHER – www.stopcocks.uk - Tel: 0800 8620010
Email: mica@stopcocks.uk

Stopcocks is a company made up of female plumbers. They arrange a free annual 'Women Installers Together Conference' in London aimed at female installers.

WOMEN ON THE TOOLS –
www.womenonthetools.org.uk
Email: info@womenonthetools.org.uk –
Mob: 07908 586339

This organisation works to promote women in the trades
that are usually dominated by men, including plumbing.
Join their mail list to find out about their events, etc.

PROFESSIONAL BODIES

CIPHE – www.ciphe.org.uk
Email: info@ciphe.org.uk – Tel: 01708 472791

The Chartered Institute of Plumbing and Heating
Engineering (CIPHE), is the professional and technical
body for the plumbing and heating industry in the UK.
The CIPHE can register members as Engineering
Technician or Incorporated Engineer with the
Engineering Council.

CIBSE – www.cibse.org
Tel: 020 8675 5211

CIBSE – Chartered Institution of Building Services
Engineers – is the standard setter and authority on
building services engineering in the UK. It publishes the
CIBSE Guides, Codes and other guidance material, which
are internationally recognised as authoritative and sets
the criteria for best practice in the profession. CIBSE can
register members as Chartered Engineer with the
Engineering Council.

CIWEM – www.ciwem.org
Tel: 020 7831 3110

The CIWEM – Chartered Institution of Water and
Environmental Management – is the only independent,
chartered professional body and registered charity with

an integrated approach to environmental, social and cultural issues.

ENGINEERING COUNCIL – www.engc.org.uk
Tel: 020 3206 0500

The Engineering Council is the UK regulatory body for the engineering profession. You'll find information on how you can register with the Engineering Council as EngTech, IEng, or CEng, when you have gained the right experience and qualifications.

ENGINEERING UK – www.engineeringuk.com
Tel: 0203 206 0400

Previously known as Engineering and Technology Board, Engineering UK promotes the vital role of engineers, engineering and technology in our society.

IDHEE – www.idhee.org.uk
Email: admin@idhee.org.uk – Tel: 01895 820954

The IDHEE – Institute of Domestic Heating and Environmental Engineers – is an independent non-profit making professional body, founded in 1964, serving the Domestic Heating Engineers. It offers courses to its members to help with their professional development.

IGEM – www.igem.org.uk
Email: general@igem.org.uk – Tel: 01509 678182

The Institution of Gas Engineers and Managers encourages its members to promote high standards and is recognised internationally as well as in the UK. IGEM has a student membership section, which is open to anyone pursuing a course of full-time or part-time study, for a qualification that satisfies the educational base requirements likely to lead to Corporate membership of the Institution.

INSTITUTE OF WATER –
www.instituteofwater.org.uk
Tel: 0191 422 0088

The Institute of Water, founded in 1945, is the only professional body that exclusively supports the careers of anyone working in the UK water sector.

SECTOR SKILLS COUNCILS

CITB – www.citb.co.uk
Tel: 0344 994 4400

The CITB is the Construction Industry Training Board and a partner in the Sector Skills Council for the construction industry in England, Scotland and Wales. It's their job to work with industry to encourage training, which helps build a safe, professional and fully qualified workforce. CITB is the largest provider of apprentices for the construction industry, with over 45 years' experience of developing skilled workers.

THE FORCES

BRITISH ARMY – www.armyjobs.mod.uk
Tel: 0345 600 8080

On this site you will find information on training to be a military engineer, which includes apprenticeships in plumbing and heating.

ROYAL NAVY – www.royalnavy.mod.uk
The Royal Navy trains Engineering Technicians who deal with a wide range of work. On the website you will find an on-line form to fill in to get information on careers.

TRADE ASSOCIATIONS

APHC – www.aphc.co.uk
Email: info@aphc.co.uk – Tel: 0121 711 5030

The Association of Plumbing and Heating Contractors (APHC) is the trade body for plumbing and heating businesses in England and Wales. The site contains information on their Competent Person Scheme.

OFTEC – www.oftec.org.uk
Tel: 01473 626298

OFTEC is a trade association that works on behalf of the oil heating and cooking industry in the UK and Republic of Ireland. It also takes a lead role in setting industry standards and manages a Competent Person Scheme for technicians who install, commission and service oil and renewable heating and cooking equipment.

SNIPEF – www.snipef.org
Email: info@snipef.org – Tel: 0131 556 0600

The Scottish and Northern Ireland Plumbing Employers' Federation is a trade association which operates in Scotland and Northern Ireland. Besides industry news and technical updates, you will find information on apprenticeships.

TRADE MAGAZINES

Trade magazines help to keep you up to date with the latest products on the market and industry news. There are numerous trade magazines that you can subscribe to, usually free of charge. Some have an on-line version. Here are just a few:

H&V News
www.hvnplus.co.uk

Heating and Plumbing Monthly (HPM)
www.hpmmag.com

Heating, Ventilating and Plumbing (HVP)
www.hvpmag.co.uk

Plumbing and Air Movement News (PHAM News) www.phamnews.co.uk

EDUCATIONAL PUBLICATIONS

ETM (Education & Training Matters) –
www.ciphe.org.uk
Email: info@ciphe.org.uk – Tel: 01708 472791

This publication is produced by the Chartered Institute of Plumbing and Heating Engineering (CIPHE). It is aimed at plumbing lecturers and is sent out to colleges and training centres three times a year (term time).

HIP MAGAZINE – www.hip-magazine.co.uk
Email: info@sng-publishing.co.uk – Tel: 0870 774 3049

This magazine is aimed at plumbing trainees and is delivered to final year plumbing students via their college, each term. However, for a small subscription, which covers postage, you can have this magazine delivered to your home. You can download back issues from their website and can access answers to the set exercises.

OTHER USEFUL ORGANISATIONS

CONSTRUCTION SKILLS CERTIFICATION SCHEME – www.cscs.uk.com
Tel: 0344 994 4777

CSCS cards confirm you have the correct training and qualifications for the type of work you carry out. You can apply for a Trainee CSCS card if you are on an NVQ Level 2 or 3 course.

COPPER INITIATIVE – www.copperplumbing.org.uk
Email: info@copperalliance.org.uk

The Copper Initiative provides technical information on the correct use of copper for pipework services in buildings. Their technical publications, electronic media and CD can be used by college lecturers, students and experienced plumbers.

JOINT INDUSTRY BOARD – www.jib-pmes.org.uk
Email: info@jib-pmes.org.uk – Tel: 01480 476925

This is the registration body for the plumbing and heating industry. There is a special section for trainees and apprentices. The website also gives information on the annual skills competition – SkillPLUMB.

LEAD SHEET TRAINING ACADEMY
www.leadsheet.co.uk
Tel: 01622 872432

The Lead Sheet Training Academy is at the forefront of training for those using lead or hard metals in the construction industry. You will find information on specialist lead courses on this website, including welding and decorative castings.

MICROGENERATION CERTIFICATION SCHEME
www.microgenerationcertification.org
Contact the helpdesk on 020 7090 1082

Visit this site for information on the different organisations running the Microgeneration Certification Scheme.

PRINCE'S TRUST – www.princes-trust.org.uk
Email: info@princes-trust.org.uk – Tel: 0800 842 842
(Regional telephone numbers on the website)

The Prince's Trust is a wonderful organisation. On the website you'll find information about personal development courses that will help to build your confidence. The Prince's Trust helps people between 14-30 years of age and even has advice on starting your own business.

WATERSAFE – www.watersafe.org.uk
Email: info@watersafe.org.uk – Tel: 0333 207 9030
WaterSafe is a dedicated on-line search facility for the general public, bringing together thousands of qualified contractors employed by plumbing businesses from the seven existing Approved Contractors' Schemes across the UK.

WORLD PLUMBING COUNCIL
www.worldplumbing.org
The World Plumbing Council (WPC) is an international organisation, which aims to develop and promote the image and standards of the plumbing industry worldwide.

THE WORSHIPFUL COMPANY OF PLUMBERS
www.plumberscompany.org.uk
Tel: 020 7628 8880
Email: clerk@plumberscompany.org.uk
The Worshipful Company of Plumbers is a Livery Company with a history going back to 1365. This organisation is still very active today and has a charitable trust that awards bursaries to plumbing students.

WRAS – www.wras.co.uk
Email: info@wras.co.uk – Tel: 0333 207 9030
The Water Regulations Advisory Scheme website has lots of useful information and advice for plumbers. It also has a detailed list of approved products and materials.

25670816R00064

Printed in Great Britain
by Amazon